750

Seventy-five Years of
Texas History

Seventy-five Years

the texas state

Senator Jack Hightower, Association Director Joe B. Frantz, and Association Pres dent Dorman H. Winfrey, with Senate Concurrent Resolution No. 38 commendi the Texas State Historical Association for its work in preserving and making ava able the history of Texas.

# of Texas History

historical association, 1897-1972

Dorman H. Winfrey

JENKINS PUBLISHING CO.
Austin / 1975

For

Dr. H. Bailey Carroll

who made many things possible

for the

Texas State Historical Association

and for me.

Contents

Introduction

Mr. Association

I have never bothered my crowded, clouded mind with my lack of belief in predestination and in reincarnation. But every now and then something happens or someone appears who makes me wonder.

Such a person is Dorman Winfrey, who I would swear was predestined to become president of the Texas State Historical Association and director of the Texas State Library, and who I would also swear must have appeared in a previous life as George Pierce Garrison, Francis R. Lubbock, or one of the other founders of the Association. For if any man living has a claim on being the embodiment of the Association, it has to be Winfrey. The late Eugene C. Barker, the late Walter Prescott Webb, and the later H. Bailey Carroll all took turns as director, and though Barker's output in the field of Texas history was prodigious, only Carroll of that trio approached a oneness with the Association. Certainly the current director does not qualify.

But in the twelve years that Winfrey worked with the

Association, he explored its outer limits fore and aft. He immersed himself in the lore of the Association; in many ways he *was* the Association. As he proved himself from the days of being a raw freshman engaged in part-time activity at the Association until he began to move outward and upward in his professional career, Carroll entrusted him with more and more of the Association's affairs. He knew the old-timers, he welcomed the new ones, he was ready always to serve and promote and visit, he proofread the galleys for *The Southwestern Historical Quarterly* (we need you now, Dorman!), he supervised annual meetings, and he shepherded Junior Historians all over the state.

But eventually limitations of the Association made it necessary for him to leave if he were going to be fair to himself professionally. What happened after that is a matter of statistics, with each rung of his upward-pointing ladder providing another case history of public service. Yet through all his years of busyness as state archivist, The University of Texas archivist, and director of the far-flung Texas State Library, Winfrey has always found time to continue serving the Association and its membership. I personally have never called on him that he wasn't right there, despite statewide demands by legislators and self-appointed VIPs, by the blind (which some critics will argue equates with legislators), with genealogists (who demand and get Saturday openings for them alone), with the federal government (which uses the library to pass out funds to public libraries and as a regional documents repository), and with plain ordinary citizens who just want to wander in and look at the murals and visit.

Away back in 1948 Walter P. Webb wrote in the *Quarterly* that "The cheerful Dorman Winfrey is the general factotum [of the Association] who does about everything any of the others ask him to do, does it cheerfully and well." More than a quarter-century later, that tribute from Texas' greatest historian still has currency, for over the years Winfrey has become the oak against which the Association often leans.

As every bromide hunter knows, Leo Durocher once coined a future *cliche* when he said, "Nice guys finish last." Dorman Winfred is living proof that Durocher's remark has its occasional magnificent exception. Although Winfrey was and is one of the world's gentlemen, he has finished first in so many Texas hearts that the state, vast though it is, is barely large enough to contain them all.

Joe B. Frantz
Austin, Texas

Seventy-five Years of Texas History

the texas state historical association, 1897-1972

by Dorman H. Winfrey *

*Speech delivered Friday, March 10, 1972, at the Annual Meeting of the Texas State Historical Association, Sheraton-Fort Worth Hotel, Fort Worth, Texas.

L ast week, on March 2, the Texas State Historical Association rounded out a full seventy-five years of its life. I think we could call this event a diamond jubilee—certainly the Association is among the very finest jewels in historical organizations in these United States. In this diamond jubilee year our thoughts might well go back seventy-five years to another jubilee celebration—that of Queen Victoria—a great "festival of empire"—which was then being observed in many parts of the world to commemorate the longest reign in English history. William McKinley was inaugurated as President of the United States that year, and Charles A. Culberson was in the Governor's Mansion in Austin. Some other significant events in 1897 included the opening of the main building of the Library of Congress, the Klondike Gold Rush to the Canadian Yukon, and publication of H. G. Wells' *The Invisible Man* and Paul Dreiser's "On the Banks of the Wabash." In New York City that year—several decades before radio became a household word—Milton Cross was born on April 16. When network radio came to America in the 1920's Cross would be identified with radio announcing and in the 1930's to the present would become "Mr. Opera" of the Saturday afternoon Metropolitan Opera radio broadcasts. On June 21, 1897, in Milan, Italy, a thirty-year-old musician, Arturo Toscanini, married Carla dei Martini. Fifty-three years later on the weekend of a Texas State Historical Association meeting in Austin, the octogenarian conductor led the NBC Symphony in a concert during its transcontinental tour. Looking back on seventy-five years of history, our minds can hardly comprehend so much that has come about in the British Empire, the United States, the State of Texas, and our own Texas State Historical Association.

A few members know some of the background of the Association's early history—that back in 1897 on the evening of February 13 "a number of gentlemen interested in Texas history met in one of the rooms of the University of Texas [established only fourteen years earlier in 1883] to discuss the organization of a State Historical Association."[1] The result was a letter of invitation, drawn up and mailed to 250 influential citizens of the state. Less than a month later, the Association was founded, appropriately, on the evening of March 2, the sixty-first anniversary of the signing of the Texas Declaration of Independence. Some two dozen persons attended the called organizational meeting held in the office of the Commissioner of Agriculture, Insurance, Statistics, and History in the State Capitol and elected ex-governor O. M. Roberts, president; George P. Garrison, recording secretary and librarian; and Lester G. Bugbee, corresponding secretary and treasurer.

Two interesting events took place on that evening of the birth of the Association. The capitol lights were operated by an individual capitol light plant and the meeting was still going on past the closing hour of the plant. The lights in the room went out and the remaining business was hurriedly transacted by the light of two lanterns that were procured from the janitor. By the light of two lanterns the Texas State Historical Association was born.[2]

The more significant event that evening—and what may have caused the session to extend beyond lights out—was a brief encounter in the battle for women's liberation. Among the twenty to thirty persons present were three women identified with historical activities, Mrs. Dora Fowler Arthur, Mrs. Julia Lee Sinks, and Mrs. Bride Neill Taylor. The latter of the trio later recalled events that evening in a paper published in 1929.[3]

. . . A . . . notable feature of the meeting was the presence of . . .. three women . . . I say "notable" advisedly, for it was by no means a thing to be expected that we should be there. Public meetings in those days were thought of as men's meetings. . . . But . . . Dr. Garrison was a forward-looking man and had sensed among the signs of the times that women were about to take their place in the intellectual and political world.

He was reading Article III of the proposed constitution, which had to do with membership: "The Association shall consist of members, life members and honorary life members." He paused, and the chair asked for possible amendments, not really expecting any. There was silence for a moment or two; then Colonel Ford spoke up with: "I move to insert the words, 'lady members' after the word 'members.' "

The secretary looked disturbed. He waited. So did the chair. . . . Dr. Garrison finally glanced toward us women with pleading in his eye. Colonel Ford, in the meantime, was indignantly calling on the chair to put his motion to vote. Now, Dr. Garrison was the gentlest of men, . . . but he simply could not stand for the proffered amendment. His silent appeal to us, however, put us in a position of embarrassment. An innovation indeed it would be for a woman to get up and speak in a man's meeting. So we sat immovable. We were seated together in a row a little to one side . . . Colonel Ford was just opposite us. . . . Again he urged on the chair. The secretary's face grew desperate in its pleading. . . . So, because the situation simply had to be saved, I finally rose and . . . ventured with: "Mr. Chairman, . . . as for myself, I feel sure that I shall find no difficulty in becoming a member of the proposed association under the section as it stands. For does not the word 'member' include both sexes?" But my effort to placate the colonel had the opposite effect. "Madam," he burst out at me furiously, "your brass may get you into the association, but you will never have the right to get in under that section as it stands." . . . I do not remember that I specially resented his flinging the word "brass" at me. I felt myself that I was brassy.

The amendment was put after this exchange of contending ideas, and lost unanimously.

3

dorman h. winfrey

The reading of the constitution proceeded.

"Section b, Fellows," read the secretary. "Members who show by published work special aptitude for historical investigation may become fellows." Here Colonel Ford interrupted again. "Doctor, I don't like that word 'fellows.'" "What is your objection, Colonel?" asked the secretary. "Well, we are going to have lady members, it seems. Now, suppose one of these lady members should do something in the history line, how would it sound to call a lady a fellow."

With the most beautiful tact, Dr. Garrison explained that . . . the word had an honorable, ancient, technical meaning, and without further pause (the chair hearing no other suggestion) he went on reading.

But to be thus ignored was more than the colonel could stand. As I look back now, it is plain to me that his suggestion was offered as a sort of olive branch to us women in atonement for the brusqueness of his rebuke to me for having presumed to contradict his first amendment, and the assembly's silent refusal to consider it was a blow to him. So, when the secretary took up his reading without more ado, the colonel rose, grumbling his indignation audibly, and went stumping out of the room, the loud strokes of his big stick as it hit the tiled floor emphasizing his disapproval of us at every step down the long corridor outside, and, far from finding the incident funny, there was not, I assure you, so much as a single smile among us. Everyone there present was too conscious that the colonel's adverse opinion of our movement would give it a serious setback with the people of the State to see anything humorous in it.

Fortunately for the Association and Texas history this event had a happy ending! A delegation was sent to confer with Colonel Ford. He became a charter member and later gave his papers to the Association.

The early lists of members of the Association contained most distinguished names and read like a Texas *Who's Who* for that day. The Association issued a *Report of the Organization of the Texas State Historical Associa-*

tion showing 124 charter members and by the end of the first year the *Quarterly* had listed the names of 416 members. As one would expect there were the veterans of the Texas Revolution, Mexican War, and Civil War; and there were Indian fighters and Texas Rangers; and at least seven names had been or would be identified with the governorship—O. M. Roberts, F. R. Lubbock, C. A. Culberson, James S. Hogg, S. W. T. Lanham, R. B. Hubbard, and Joseph D. Sayers. The membership included many lawyers as well as members of the state legislature, Supreme Court, and the national Congress; a large number of college and university presidents and members of the governing boards of educational institutions; religious figures and newspaper editors; and a most impressive number of school superintendents.

Early members included writers and publishers such as James T. De Shields, Noah Smithwick, Mrs. Percy V. Pennybacker, A. H. Belo, Dudley G. Wooten, and H. P. N. Gammel; national political figures like John H. Reagan, Albert Sidney Burleson, Edward M. House, and David F. Houston; and state Grange leaders, A. J. Rose and George C. Pendleton. Sir Swante Palm and John A. Lomax were among the collectors of books and ballads. Librarians included C. W. Raines and Elizabeth Howard West, and among the geologists were Robert T. Hill and E. T. Dumble. Fortunately, I suppose, President John Garland James of the Agricultural and Mechanical College of Texas and President George T. Winston of the University of Texas both took out memberships that first year. The Baptists were represented by Rufus C. Burleson and the Episcopalians by Bishop George H. Kinsolving. Two persons closely identified with founding the Daughters of the Republic, Miss Hally Ballinger Bryan and Mrs. Rebecca J. Fisher, were among the very first Association members, as was Mrs. Bride Neill Taylor, founder of the American History Club in Austin in 1893, and first president of that organization. Another charter member, Adele B. Looscan served as president from 1915 to 1925. The bar could claim members Joseph Weldon Bailey, O. W. Williams, Robert S. Gould, and John Charles Townes, while the business world was represented by Charles Schreiner and George W. Brackenridge. Members associated with famous Texans included Mrs. Anson Jones, the widow of the last president of the Republic; Sam Houston's daughter, Mrs. Nettie Houston Bringhurst; Julia Pease, daughter of E. M. Pease; and two San Antonio sisters who would hold membership in the Association for more than half a century, Mary and Adina de Zavala, granddaughters of Lorenzo de Zavala. Scholars and educators included Professor of Classics William J. Battle and Daniel A. Penick, who had a strong reputation as a Greek scholar and tennis coach; pioneer anthropologist James E. Pearce; and historians Isaac J. Cox, Walter F. McCaleb, and "Eugene C. Barker, Esq. from Palestine." From Blanco the Honorable J. W. Baines, grandfather of a future President, sent in a membership and later A. W. Moursund from Fredericksburg joined. Many of the names identified with the early membership and growth of our Association have lasting meaning to Texas and its history and are generally known among historical gatherings such as ours.

There are also some names less instantly recognizable but equally distinguished among the charter members of the Association. Such members were Dr. J. W. Carhart who "invented the automobile, an accomplishment later recognized by the American Manufacturer's Association;"[4] Texas Ranger John Washington Darlington who participated in the Plum Creek Fight; James Luther Slayden, president of the American Peace Society and original trustee for Carnegie Endowment for International Peace; Dr. Allen John Smith whose research established the hookworm as endemic in this country; and Dillard Ruker Fant, cattleman who in 1884 drove 42,000 head of cattle from Texas to Wyoming.

What.a solid and broad foundation of membership on which the Association could grow. The next year, members would include artist H. A. McArdle, Houston's William Marsh Rice, and Judge A. W. Terrell. Year after year the Association membership would grow[5] and recruit not only the writers but the makers of Texas history.

Some of the early members have descendants who still have Association memberships; Mrs. Emma Holmes Jenkins at Bastrop was the great grandmother of Association Fellow John Holmes Jenkins, III, and J. D. Matlock was an uncle of Joseph Dixon Matlock, Association life member. Governor Hogg's daughter, Miss Ima, continues that family's membership. Among the charter members were two noted Austin doctors, Joe S. Wooten and his son, Thomas D. Wooten. Today a descendant, Dr. Greenwood S. Wooten, Jr., carrying on a family tradition of medicine and membership in the Association, has his Austin office in a historic and now restored building at 107 East 10th Street. On the doctor's wall are pictures of his grandfather and great grandfather, along with pictures of his great uncles, Dr. Goodall Harrison Wooten and Dudley Goodall Wooten, second president of the Association and author of the two-volume *Comprehensive History of Texas, from 1685 to 1897* (1898). Thus the torch continues from generation to generation, its flames showing no signs of fading.

But an era did close recently for the Association's first seventy-five years. The last surviving charter member, Judge James W. McClendon of Austin, died on January 9, at the age of 98.

The first annual meeting was held on June 17, 1897, in Austin, and President O. M. Roberts talked on "The Proper Work of the Association."[6] He pointed out the objects of the Association as stated in the constitution," . . . the promotion of historical studies; and, in particular, the discovery, collection, preservation, and publication of historical material, especially such as related to Texas."

dorman h. winfrey

Roberts commented: "Its objects are not so much to induce the writing of a connected and complete history as to furnish the facts for that object in the future." The facts of Texas history would go into the *Quarterly* and this publication became "the cornerstone upon which the entire framework of the organization's achievements were laid."[7]

Many of the early officers and members of the Association had made the history of Texas and on the pages of the *Quarterly* they would record for posterity what they knew. And this they did with original letters, diaries, journals, and memories. These *Quarterly* articles, covering every aspect of the state's history, do indeed constitute the very "spirit of Texas history."[8]

To illustrate with just one example, one can look at the *Quarterly* articles and references credited to the names of Valentine Bennet and Miles S. Bennet.[9] The elder Bennet—a participant in such events as Velasco, Concepcion, siege of Bexar, Texan-Santa Fe Expedition, and Somervell Expedition—gave the classic description of the official uniform of the Texas Revolution: "Rags, sir, just rags; nine out of every ten soldiers who fought in the Texas Revolution wore this same uniform, and sire, it was a fighting uniform." On the pages of the *Quarterly*, son Miles S. Bennet, an early member of the Association, describes accompanying his father to the early veteran's reunions and touring with him the places "made historic by the movements of the colonists and the events of the battle and retreat."

Bennet listened to what was said. "Although these incidents were considered of small importance at the time, I like to recall them and place them on record, that they not be completely forgotten." Bennet's article in the *Quarterly* ("The Battle of Gonzales, The 'Lexington' of the Texas Revolution") has preserved much Revolutionary history that would have been lost in a few years.

The excellent material for the *Quarterly* articles then as today came in largely from the papers prepared for and read at the annual meetings. A sampling of the early papers would include Dudley G. Wooten, "The Life and Services of Oran Milo Roberts," C. W. Raines, "Enduring Laws of the Republic of Texas," John H. Reagan, "The Closing Hours of the Confederacy," Mrs. Percy V. Pennybacker, "What the Texas Teacher Can Do for Texas History," George P. Garrison, "Another Texas Flag," and Eugene C. Barker, "The Difficulties of a Mexican Revenue Officer." Association President T. G. Harwood—taking inventory at the time the organization was thirty years old—commented:

> There is no daily newspaper, no magazine, no book, yet written by a Texan or about Texas, that makes as permanent a record and one so sure to be preserved for all time to come as the *Quarterly*. It has necessarily become the foundation of an history; and names written on its pages will be known when many other more-pretentious publications, more expensive epitaphs, have been erased by time.[10]

President Harwood also paid attention to the fortunate circumstances of the Association "having been born" in the University of Texas and "being sponsored by its professors of history—otherwise it would probably have languished and died with the old Texans who fathered and mothered it."

Exactly thirty years earlier (July, 1897), the *Texas Magazine*, one of the early literary magazines for the state, noted the inauguration of the Texas State Historical Association and its *Quarterly* with this comment and prediction: "The interest shown (by officers and members) has been most intelligent and enthusiastic, and there is no doubt the work of the body will become one of the most important and valuable that can be done for Texas."[11]

For seventy-five years now, the valuable *Quarterly* articles—marked by accuracy and scholarship—have been

dorman h. winfrey

referred to again and again by all writers of Texas history. Today few persons would question the statement that the *Quarterly* is the most important single source of Texas history, and the authors of most Texas history books cite the *Quarterly* more heavily than any single source.

In 1949 Joseph Norman Heard, graduate student at the University of Texas at Austin for a study "Preservation and Publication of Texana by the Texas State Historical Association" (MA. UT, 1951), conducted a survey among some forty editors of various state historical journals to rank the ten journals "which in their judgment best carried out the objectives of a state historical society." In the survey Heard found that few state historical society journals are considered by qualified historians to be on a par with the *Southwestern Historical Quarterly*, and that the *Quarterly* ranked "as one of the two journals in the nation which best carry out the objectives of a state historical society."[12] In the words of the late Walter Prescott Webb, "the files of the *Quarterly* comprise a contribution to scholarship unsurpassed in any field."[13]

Along with the production of "historical matter" in the *Quarterly*, the early Association officers and members were equally interested in the discovery, collection, and preservation of the sources of Texas history. That first called meeting on February 13, 1897, had stressed the great urgency to stop the destruction of the records of Texas history, and urged that an organization be formed within thirty days. A strong effort was made immediately, through a plea in the *Quarterly*, "to ascertain the present location, ownership, condition, etc., of the vast mass of MSS. now in the hands of private persons in Texas, and, if possible, to secure for the Association possession of the originals. . . . Private diaries, family letters, journals of travel, old newspapers, genealogical notices, etc., etc., are of quite as much value in recovering the history of Texas as are State papers and public documents."

That first year of its existence the officers of the Association urged that Texas source materials be collected and kept in Texas. The *Quarterly* made this observation:

> "Is it seeming, is it not discreditable to the people of Texas, that they should leave the collection of material for the history of the State to the great endowed Northern libraries, so that her own citizens, when they wish to learn of her past, must go to Boston, or New York, or Madison? Shall outsiders be permitted to lead in perpetuating the memory of the patient endurance and heroic deeds of those who builded the republic? It is to be hoped that the neglect so long shown the graves of Houston and of Rusk will not be reflected in popular forgetfulness or disregard of their public services. Let Texas arouse herself for very shame, and begin at once the discharge of her filial duty."[14]

And Association members did respond to the plea in the *Quarterly*. The Texas Veteran's Association turned over its archives as a gift to the University of Texas. Mrs. Julia Lee Sinks of Giddings gave a valuable scrapbook "full of important historical matter." Judge Beauregard Bryan presented a pamphlet by Ashbel Smith, *Reminiscences of the Texas Republic* (1876), and artist H. A. McArdle sent in a letter written by Captain Robert M. Potter. Mrs. Anson Jones gave a "valuable collection of newspapers and relics," Judge C. W. Raines presented a "scrapbook containing a copy of the diary of Dr. J. H. Barnard." William P. Devereux in Jacksonville sent the Association "two interesting old newspapers," while his mother, Mrs. Sarah Garrison, contributed a copy of the La Grange *Intelligencer* for July 4, 1844. Other valuable collections given to the Association during those early years included the Bexar Archives, the Austin Papers, and the O. M. Roberts Papers.[15] Lester G. Bugbee was instrumental in securing the Bexar Archives, while Guy M. Bryan, Association vice-president and nephew of Stephen F. Austin, made a gift of the Austin Papers.

Valuable Texana also came from outside the state. Will

M. Tipton in Santa Fe, New Mexico, contributed "the original Order Book of the Santa Fe Expedition." In sending the gift Tipton wrote: "I shall take great pleasure in presenting it to the Texas State Historical Association, where I feel that after its wanderings of fifty-eight years it is entitled to a resting place." This rare document, along with the others given to the Association and later transferred to the University of Texas Library, is now in the University of Texas Archives and is recorded as item number 1889 in Chester Kielman's *The University of Texas Archives: A Guide to the Historical Collections in the University of Texas Library* (1967).

In 1947 the Association was fifty years old and the Director at that time, Dr. H. Bailey Carroll, wrote: "The heritage of the past must be matched by contributions of the present to meet the challenge of the future."[16] Dr. Carroll, with some thirty years service to the Association, is credited with pioneering the Junior Historian movement and placing the Association on a sound financial footing. Working with Leslie Waggener, Jr., and a dedicated Ways and Means Committee of the Association, Dr. Carroll saw an endowment become a reality, almost fifty years after the recommendation had first come from an Executive Council back in 1899.

At the "Golden Jubilee" dinner in 1947 the Honorable C. Stanley Banks, Sr., spoke and observed that our organization was strong, well established and recognized in the ranks of scholarly societies. But much of the Association's first 50 years can best be described as "an uphill struggle." Nearly all the early work done by Garrison and Bugbee was voluntary and as an additional chore to other university duties. Bugbee, who died at the age of 32, is credited with supporting the *Quarterly* out of his own pocket in addition to the extra time he spent—summer vacations included—in soliciting members. At the time of Garrison's death on July 3, 1910, he was engaged in editing *Quarterly* copy from his sick bed.

Mr. Banks mentioned that there "are two things we

ought to learn from history: one, that we are not in ourselves superior to our fathers: another [and I was not sure back then that I agreed with or understood what Mr. Banks was saying], that we are shamefully and monstrously inferior to them [our fathers] if we do not advance beyond them." Mr. Banks concluded by saying: "The torch of Texas History is now in our hands: while we hold it, may it shine brightly: and then when we pass it on, may we do so with the same historical zeal as did Garrison and Bugbee and all of the others."[17]

I mentioned that twenty-five years ago, I was not certain that I agreed with or understood what Mr. Banks was saying when he stated that "we are shamefully and monstrously inferior to them [our forefathers] if we do not advance beyond them." Four persons closely identified with the work of the Association then were present and heard Mr. Banks' speech. These were Professors Eugene C. Barker, H. Bailey Carroll, Walter P. Webb, and Mrs. Coral H. Tullis, all members of the University of Texas history department. These persons, as we all know, greatly advanced the work and prestige of the Association after Bugbee, Garrison, Charles W. Ramsdell, and others passed on; they substantiate now in my mind what Mr. Banks said then.

If Professors Barker, Webb, Carroll, and Mrs. Tullis had not gone beyond Garrison, Bugbee, Ramsdell and others in the Association's work, then this organization would be without a book auction at the Annual Meeting, would never have had a "Texas Collection" section of the *Quarterly*, would not have developed the Junior Historian program, and would never have undertaken a book publication program that included the monumental *Handbook of Texas*. Happily, under our present Director, Joe B. Frantz, we have seen impressive growth and commendable changes the past few years: a new and most attractive format for the *Quarterly*, a "Riding Line" publication, a revitalized Junior Historian program, and annual and midyear meetings held in

dorman h. winfrey

various parts of the state. This is the type progress an organization should witness from year to year, from decade to decade, from generation to generation, yea, even from jubilee to jubilee. And what about the next twenty-five years and the centennial anniversary of this Association? Well, my term of office is almost over and the Executive Council has not authorized me to issue invitations for our meetings in 1997. I will, however, make a prediction for the next quarter of a century. The Association will grow and surpass the accomplishments of the last seventy-five years.[18] With what we in the Texas State Historical Association have inherited from the labor of others during the last three-quarters of a century, we ought to be able to do even more than has been done by those who have gone on before us. David F. Houston, one of our most illustrious presidents—President of Texas A&M, the University of Texas, and Secretary of Agriculture under Woodrow Wilson—said to this Association in 1908: "We are only at the beginning." I would hope that in 1997, the membership of the Association will look back and say of us, "They were only at the beginning." Continued growth and undreamed of accomplishments must take place. Otherwise our generation will be "shamefully and monstrously inferior" to Garrison, Bugbee, Barker, Carroll, Webb, and Mrs. Tullis and others "if we do not advance beyond them."

footnotes

1. "A Report of the Organization of the Texas State Historical Association," *Quarterly of the Texas State Historical Association*, I (July, 1897), p. 1.

2. "A Half-Century of the Texas State Historical Association," *Southwestern Historical Quarterly* (Extra Number), February 1, 1947.

3. Mrs. Bride Neill Taylor, "The Beginnings of the State Historical Association," *Southwestern Historical Quarterly*, XXXIII, (July, 1929), pp. 1-17.

4. W. P. Webb and H. Bailey Carroll (eds.), *The Handbook of Texas*, Vol. I, p. 296.

5. David F. Houston, "The Texas State Historical Association and Its Work," *Quarterly of the Texas State Historical Association*, XI (April, 1908), 245. By October of 1899 the number had reached 710. At that time Austin with 132 members had more than twice as many persons in the Association as did San Antonio with 63. Houston counted 40 members, Dallas 33, and Waco 19. In the western part of the state El Paso had 7 members. The membership was distributed in 178 Texas localities, "besides 24 members in sixteen other States." In 1908 membership was "over two thousand."

6. O. M. Roberts, "The Proper Work of the Association," *Quarterly of Texas State Historical Association*, I (July, 1897), p. 3. The Association may be the only historical group to hold an annual meeting so soon after organizing. The Executive Council met on May 28, 1897, and anxious and enthusiastic to get things going arranged for the first annual meeting to be held on June 17, during commencement at the University of Texas.

A midwinter meeting of the Association was held that first year in San Antonio, at Turner Hall, on December 29, 1897. The second annual meeting of the Association was held in Austin on June 16th and 17th, 1898, two days following commencement graduation of the University of Texas. The *Quarterly* noted that "The railroads of the State have agreed to give a rate of one fare and one-third for the round trip, and the tickets will be sold under such conditions that those who wish can attend both the commencement and the meeting of the Association." The *Quarterly* editor felt that the Association "meetings do much to arouse and stimulate enthusiasm, and all that can possibly come are urged to be present."

Midwinter meetings were held in Huntsville on January 9 and 10, 1900, and at Baylor University in Waco on January 5, 1901. Annual Association meetings held at the University of Texas following commencement became unsatisfactory "mainly for the reason that all those who attend the Commencement exercises—as most of the members in Austin do—have little energy left for the meetings of the Association." This was solved in 1901 by moving the meeting date to April 22. And the next two annual meetings were held on April 21, 1902, and April 21, 1903, jointly with the Texas Veteran's Association and the Daughters of the Republic of Texas at Lampasas and Waco. Cooperation and unity with such groups meant strength for the Association.

7. Joseph Norman Heard, "Preservation and Publication of Texana by the Texas State Historical Association" (M.A. Thesis, University of Texas, 1951), p. 15. In 1912 the *Quarterly* title was changed to *Southwestern Historical Quarterly*.

dorman h. winfrey

8. *Southwestern Historical Quarterly*, XLII (April, 1939), 391.
9. See Miles S. Bennet, "The Battle of Gonzales, The 'Lexington' of the Texas Revolution," *Quarterly of the Texas State Historical Association*, II, (April, 1899), p. 313-316; Adele B. Looscan, "Miles Squier Bennet," *ibid.*, VII (October, 1903), 167-168; Marie Bennet Urwitz, "Valentine Bennet," *ibid.*, IX (January, 1906), 145-156.
10. T. F. Harwood, "Review of the Work of the Texas State Historical Association," *Southwestern Historical Quarterly*, XXXI (July, 1927), 32.
11. *The Texas Magazine*, III (July, 1897), 42.
12. Heard, "Preservation and Publication of Texana by the Texas State Historical Association, 39.
13. W. P. Webb, "Salute to Youth" Editorial, *The Junior Historian*, I (January, 1941). Mrs. Coral H. Tullis (comp.), "Publications of the Texas· State Historical Association, July, 1897, through April, 1937," *Southwestern Historical Quarterly*, XLI (July, 1937), 3-82.
14. "The Affairs of the Association," *Quarterly of the Texas State Historical Association*, I (October, 1897), 131.
15. H. Bailey Carroll, "The Texas State Historical Association," The *Library Chronicle of The University of Texas*, IV (Fall, 1950), 20.
16. "A Half-Century of the Texas State Historical Association," *Southwestern Historical Quarterly* (Extra Number), February 1, 1947.
17. C. Stanley Banks, Sr., "Address . . . on the occasion of the 50th Anniversary Dinner of the Texas State Historical Association Held March 25, 1947, at Stephen F. Austin Hotel in Austin, Texas," Archives Collection, University of Texas Library, Austin, Texas. The early years of the Association's history can best be described as "an uphill struggle." Nearly all the early work done by Garrison and Bugbee was voluntary and as an additional chore to other University duties. Bugbee, who died at the age of thirty-two, is credited with supporting the *Quarterly* out of his own pocket in addition to the extra time he spent—summer vacations included—in soliciting members. Bugbee's contributions have been recorded by Eugene C. Barker in *Lester Gladstone Bugbee: A Memorial* (Austin, Texas State Historical Association, 1945). At the time of Garrison's death on July 3, 1910, he was engaged in editing *Quarterly* copy from his sick bed. During the early years Eugene C. Barker and E. W. Winkler did clerical work on the *Quarterly* and Barker was paid $8.75 commission "on securing advertisements." Barker, while a University of Texas student, had been a mail clerk on the night run of the Houston and Texas Central Railroad from Austin to Houston, and the early issues of the *Quarterly* carried as many as four pages of advertisements for Texas railroads. Much valuable Association history and news of early members appears in the "Notes

and Documents" and "Affairs of the Association" sections of the *Quarterly*. Members learned of the appointment of Judge C. W. Raines to the position of state librarian ("thoroughly fitted for the place and loves the work and will do it well"); the appointment of Eugene C. Barker as tutor in history and E. W. Winkler as fellow ("the appointments are both well deserved"); that Walter F. McCaleb, awarded a "traveling fellowship by the University of Chicago" and I. J. Cox of the San Antonio Academy spent the summer of 1898 touring Mexico ("on bicycles while doing historical research"); and that Professor Garrison would offer a graduate history course in 1898-99 on 'The Texas Revolution."

18. Joe B. Frantz, "History Looking Ahead: the Present and Future of the Texas State Historical Association," *Southwestern Historical Quarterly*, LXX (January, 1967), 353-371.

A Bridge Between Generations

*the junior historians of the
texas state historical association*

*by Dorman H. Winfrey**

*Speech given Saturday, November 27, 1971, in Jefferson, Texas, at a joint meeting of the Texas State Historical Association and Harrison County Historical Survey Committee.

Building the Bridge

*by Will Allen Dromgoole**

An old man, going a lone highway,
Came, at the evening, cold and gray,
To a chasm, vast, and deep, and wide,
Through which was flowing a sullen tide.

The old man crossed in the twilight dim;
The sullen stream had no fears for him;
But he turned, when safe on the other side,
And built a bridge to span the tide.

"Old man," said a fellow pilgrim, near,
"You are wasting strength with building here;
Your journey will end with the ending day;
You never again must pass this way;
You have crossed the chasm, deep and wide,—
Why build you the bridge at the eventide?"

The builder lifted his old gray head:
"Good friend, in the path I have come," he said,
"There followeth after me today
A youth, whose feet must pass this way.

This chasm, that has been naught to me,
To that fair-haired youth may a pitfall be.
He, too, must cross in the twilight dim;
Good friend, I am building the bridge for him."

Early students and teachers of Texas history were bridge builders. Nearly a hundred years ago this poem, "Building the Bridge," was written by Will Allen Dromgoole. It is not generally known that this author was a woman and that she was a teacher in old Salado College in Bell County. —Pat Ireland Nixon

Junior Historian, September, 1948.

We hear a good bit these days about the generation gap and the great distance of misunderstanding between adults and young persons in nearly every aspect of life, living, and culture.

One area in Texas where this does not exist is in Texas history. And this is probably due in large part to an event which took place in the Texas State Historical Association in 1939.

There were many important events that year. In international news were headlines concerning the end of the Spanish Civil War with the surrender of the loyalists, the visit of King George VI and Queen Elizabeth to the United States, the opening of World's Fairs in both New York and San Francisco (with exhibits from nearly all the countries of the world except Nazi Germany), and the outbreak of World War II with Germany's invasion of Poland on September 1.

There were some other significant events happening also. The three branches of the Methodist church were reunited after 109 years of division, and the first regular transatlantic passenger air service began operation between New York and Lisbon, Portugal (Pan American Airways' Dixie Clipper crossed the Atlantic with 22 passengers in slightly less than 24 hours). The best selling book that year was *The Grapes of Wrath*, by John Steinbeck, (a novel of the "Okies" who had been dispossessed by dust storms in 1934) and numerous Academy Awards were handed out to the most successful money making movie of all time, "Gone with the

dorman h. winfrey

Wind." "Grandma Moses" became famous overnight with her paintings in the Unknown American Painters Exhibition. Nylon stockings went on sale in America for the first time. In sports National Football Champion that year was Texas A&M, coached by Homer Norton. Their record: 10 wins, no losses, no ties.

The biggest news story and perhaps the most significant event in the history of man for many centuries went unnoticed in 1939. Albert Einstein wrote to President Roosevelt that the atom could be split and that it was possible to produce an atom bomb.

Down in Austin, Texas, that year, an event took place which would later influence a few lives and certainly have importance in Texas history. Dr. Walter Prescott Webb, then director of the Texas State Historical Association, made an announcement in the "Texas Collection" section of the *Southwestern Historical Quarterly*, in October, 1939, of the beginning of a junior historian organization. Dr. Webb wrote:

> Plans are being perfected for the organization of a Junior State Historical Association among the high school students of Texas. The purpose is to stimulate the study of state and local history by high school students. The function of the Junior Historians will be to collect the history of Texas as recorded in their respective communities. They will do this by interviewing parents, early settlers, and others as to past events. They will seek to acquaint themselves with Texas history and literature and thereby develop a richer culture upon the great Texas heritage. From their membership should come the future historians of Texas.

This, then, was the first effort to build "a bridge between generations" in Texas history—the establishment of the Junior Historians of Texas.

Dr. Webb's role in founding the Junior Historians cannot be exaggerated and J. Frank Dobie remarked as early as 1942:

I don't know but when Webb gets to St. Peter, he may not have more credit there for the Junior Historians of Texas than he will have for the books he has written, because of the far-reachingness, if I may use such a word, of this Junior Historian movement can't be determined at all. . . .

For the next few minutes let us look at the Junior Historian organization during its early years, examine the *Junior Historian* magazine, and later roles of some of the Junior Historian members. In a sense, just how far has the program "reached" (to use Mr. Dobie's term) during the past thirty-two years?

By January, 1941, with 21 chapters operating in the high schools of Texas the first issue of the *Junior Historian* magazine appeared and Dr. Webb contributed the first editorial, "Salute to Youth." Dr. Webb admitted that the magazine was an experiment, just as the *Quarterly* of the Texas State Historical Association had been an experiment back in 1897. With reference to the *Junior Historian* publication, Dr. Webb commented that the purpose of the magazine

> will be to foster in young people a love of their own state by developing their knowledge of the state. We are making the experiment because we believe that Texas boys and girls are competent to collect the history, tradition and lore of their separate communities and to write out the results of their investigations in a way worthy of publication. We propose to provide an outlet for what they do in the way of historical writing.
>
> It will be the policy of the *Junior Historian* to encourage young people to investigate the past of their own community, town, or city. There are a thousand good stories hidden in the memories of older people, stories of their own recollections of younger days. There are interesting excursions to make to historic sites, to old forts, along early trails, and to the courthouse where the county's records are kept. In many homes are faded letters, diaries, or newspaper clippings which make the past glow with reality. We believe that the history of Texas is worthy of

dorman h. winfrey

preservation; we believe that the youth of Texas can and
will help preserve it. It is to the boys and girls of Texas
that the Texas State Historical Association dedicates the
Junior Historian.

The man whom Dr. Webb put in charge of the Junior
Historian organization and who guided it for more than a
quarter of a century was Dr. H. Bailey Carroll. Dr. Carroll,
with his obvious interest and manner of dress, with Stetson
hat and cigar, captured the imagination of the Junior Historians back in those days. For them he was "a combination
of cowboy Gary Cooper and John Knott's 'Old Man
Texas.'"

With leaders like Dr. Webb, Dr. Carroll, and Dr. Eugene C. Barker, at that time the dean of Texas historians and
author of *The Life of Stephen F. Austin,* and others, I
suppose it is understandable that they would have had faith
in turning over some of the research and writing of Texas
history to the youth of the state. These men knew their
Texas history and they knew that young people had a hand
in making the early history of Texas. For example, Stephen
F. Austin was 27 years old when he took over his father's
work to colonize Texas. William B. Travis had arrived in
Texas in his early 20's and died in the Alamo at the age of
26. And Charles Goodnight was only 21 years old when he
took the first steps to found the cattle industry by starting
his first cattle on their drive to markets outside the state.

Dr. Carroll wrote the second editorial for the *Junior
Historian* magazine, published in March, 1941, and commented on some of the Junior Historian philosophy:

The Texas State Historical Association is interested in re-
vealing the complete round of life in Texas. We believe
that if it was worth while to make the record, it is an honorable and essential duty to preserve it. The Junior Historian movement is designed to put its major emphasis on
youthful inquiries into the way of life in the various Texas
communities. In other words, the whole force of the
movement is directed toward developing a greater

24

knowledge of one's homeland. The importance of this arises from the fact that in an orderly succession, this knowledge is a prerequisite to a love of homeland, which in its turn is the basic essential of any worth while patriotism.

The Junior Historian movement, therefore, is creating and fostering the most sound American patriotism of which we have any knowledge.

Emphasis on the communities of Texas and upon the community life nurtured by the Texas soil brings history close to home. Such a study is entirely fitting and proper for youth. It is a necessary adjustment to his cultural heritage. The inquiry starts with simple things—necessary before one can approach the complexities of adult life.

And the simple things of Texas life include a multitude of subjects. What of the origin of the names of the creeks, rivers, lakes, ponds, and hills of the locality? Who were the first settlers? What was their background? How did they live? These things, and many others of a like nature, can be digested and understood by any reasonably careful high school student. And the pursuit of answers to problems of this type can become a fascinating game of searching for facts.

Dr. Barker contributed an editorial on "The Importance of Local History" to the *Junior Historian* magazine in January, 1942.

Junior Historians have a right to congratulate themselves upon the importance of their work in developing local history. They are helping to create the very foundations of written history because all historical movements and events are local in origin. The story of world movements is made up of a multitude of local units which the historian condenses, organizes, and fits together into a single narrative or exposition.

Figuratively speaking, Junior Historians are engaged in the useful and fascinating labor of digging the mines and tailings of past events and delivering them to master craftsmen who weave them into a unified mosaic which may picture the life of a movement, an era, or a state. Every

dorman h. winfrey

issue of the *Junior Historian* contains rich nuggets of fact
which help to illuminate the history of Texas.

In one sense, local history is the truest history that we
have. It is rarely distorted by propagandists who misin-
terpret facts in the effort to draw from history arguments
to strengthen a good or bad cause. The historian of local
affairs need never apologize for his efforts. His aim is to
discover and tell the truth for its own sake. He turns no
grindstones for the sharpening of selfish axes.

The Junior Historian program was never intended to
include every student in school, but instead was designed for
the historically minded. The program intended to develop
historians, not just to create an interest and appreciation of
Texas history, but to write history. To accomplish this, a
vehicle was needed to provide an outlet for the writings, and
the early leaders in the Texas State Historical Association
conceived the idea of a *Junior Historian* magazine. It became
the first and only magazine written exclusively by and for
young persons.

Articles in the *Junior Historian* magazine have touched
on every aspect of the state's history and have reflected all
types of research. Early newspapers, both interviews with
and old papers of early pioneers, church records, business
records, and markers in cemeteries have been utilized by the
young writers. Students have been encouraged repeatedly to
write about their local area. This accomplishes two things:
(1) Local history is preserved (2) The writer becomes better
trained in historical research and writing.

Competent historians have been amazed at the quality
of material found in the *Junior Historian* magazine and it is
surprising sometimes how frequently citations to articles in
the *Junior Historian* appear in scholarly journals. The worth
of some of those articles is demonstrated by bibliographies
in the *Handbook of Texas*, and occasionally the only
citation available is to an article in the *Junior Historian*
magazine.

Paul Horgan, today ranked as one of America's best known writers, was an early Junior Historian co sponsor of a chapter at the New Mexico Military Institute in Roswell, New Mexico. This, incidentally, was the only Junior Historian chapter located outside the state. Horgan contributed an editorial to the magazine in March, 1943, and asked the question,

> "Yes, but what shall I write about?" His answer, "Write about anything that is truly related to the land of your birth and being . . . if you can feel truly about the facts of your historical past, and if you can get that into the words for others to feel with you, you will solve the problem of what to write about, *and* how to write it. Everyone must discover the way for himself but the field is already opened up. And a magazine is waiting for your best efforts."

Horgan admitted, "A piece of writing *always* wants to be published" and he remarked, "It seems to me that the *Junior Historian* answers the question perfectly."

Another early Junior Historian sponsor was Miss Llerena Friend who later took a doctorate in history, became librarian of the Eugene C. Barker Texas History Center at the University of Texas, and wrote the award-winning book, *Sam Houston: The Great Designer*. Miss Friend's Junior Historians were tough competitors and the number of articles in the *Junior Historian* magazine from Wichita Falls is a credit to Miss Friend's guidance.

Junior Historians in the East Texas area have done a rather good job with their local research. In Henderson our Junior Historian chapter did research on and took field trips to such intersting places as Julien Devereux's Monte Verdi Plantation, Trammel's Trace, and Old Camden, ghost town on a bluff of the Sabine River, not far from here. A good many of the Junior Historian research papers dealing with East Texas topics have been printed in the *Junior Historian* magazine. Some of these articles include: "Palestine Salt

dorman h. winfrey

Works," "Early Schools in San Augustine," "The New London School Explosion," "Hog Killing Time in East Texas," "Lucy Holcombe Pickens, Queen of the Confederacy," "Jefferson, Queen of the Cypress," "The Situation of the East Texas Indians," "The Old Stone Fort," "Trammel's Trace," and "The Dogwood Trail."

The human by product of the Junior Historian organization is certainly important and something in which the Association can take more than ordinary pride. A former Junior Historian from Pascal High School in Fort Worth, Texas, Ernest May, Jr., was an early Junior Historian writer who had articles published in the magazine. Ernest took a Ph.D. in history, has had some half dozen successful books on American history published, and is now a professor of history at Harvard University. Ralph Wooster was a Junior Historian from Baytown in the Robert E. Lee Chapter who won prizes and had articles published and has gone on to write award winning books and is now Chairman of the History Department at Lamar State University. John H. Jenkins, III, a Junior Historian from Beaumont, became the youngest person ever to have a book published by the University of Texas Press in Austin. Johnny has to his credit now a half dozen books in Texas history and owns the Jenkins Publishing Company in Austin. Jenny Lind Porter did her first writing as a Junior Historian, later took a doctor's degree in English at the University of Texas, has continued to publish widely and was honored by the state legislature as poet laureate of Texas. Ruth Carolyn Byrd Winfrey did research in Marshall on Lucy Holcombe Pickens and won first place with her paper. Ruth Carolyn has continued an interest in history and holds membership in the American History Club in Austin. The list could go on.

The annual Junior Historian meeting in Austin was and still is the highlight of the school year. During the early years on the eve of World War II approximately 150 youngsters attended. Some years following World War II as many as 600 have come to Austin to read the scholarly papers, attend the awards luncheon and then take the Junior Historian tour which includes such important historical places as the Old French Legation, the State Cemetery, the Governor's Mansion, the Barker Texas History Center, the Texas Archives and Library Building, and now the Lyndon Baines Johnson Presidential Library. For many of these youngsters the annual meeting provides the first trip to the state's Capitol. Our Junior Historian chapter from Henderson made two of those trips before and during the first year of World War II. While the war was going on and tires were being rationed, the question came up about essential transportation. Was a bus trip to Austin, Texas, for a historical meeting essential to the war effort and could it be justified? Our chapter sent a request to the Office of Price Administration in Shreveport and the federal office there approved the trip. The government may have been impressed by the fact that our Junior Historian Chapter had won an award the previous December with a "Buy Defense Bonds" float in the annual Henderson Santa Claus Parade. The Junior Historian luncheon that school year held on April 11, 1942, in the Driskill Hotel, was historic in a good many ways. J. Frank Dobie, the lovable writer of much Texas history and folklore, presented the awards and gave a beautiful talk on Indian paint brushes, and J. Evetts Haley, who appeared with cowboy hat, boots, and revolvers, did some rope tricks. Those who know Evetts Haley can visualize that this individual was no phoney but was a "real" Texas rancher-cowboy and no one kidded. This may have been the last time Dobie and Haley ever appeared together on a stage. Their political views widened as the years went by. The luncheon that year in the Driskill Hotel dining room cost 75 cents.

Some young historians in the University of Texas history department assisted in the Junior Historian program during those early days. W. Turrentine Jackson served as a guide for Junior Historian tours of Austin when the annual meeting was held. Professor Jackson has done on to become

dorman h. winfrey

a nationally recognized historian and teaches at the University of California at Davis. W. Eugene Hollon was another tour guide during those early years. He is now chairman of the history department at the University of Toledo and has authored such outstanding books as: *William Bollaert's Texas, Southwest Old and New,* and *The Great American Desert.* E. C. Barksdale, Professor Emeritus and former chairman of the history department at the University of Texas at Arlington, also helped with the Junior Historian program during the early years. Dr. Ralph Steen, now president of Stephen F. Austin University in Nacogdoches, appeared on the program to give the Junior Historians solid advice in writing and research. These noted historians— along with Dr. Webb, Dr. Carroll and others—provided the very best in advice and counsel that was available for the youth of Texas.

Earlier, we gave a good bit of credit to the leaders and bridge builders of the Association and pointed out how much trust they had in Texas youth. I think we have been able to understand how their good judgment and careful planning three decades ago avoided a gap in Texas history.

Less than two years ago another look was taken at the Junior Historian program and Dr. Joe B. Frantz and his associates took steps to make sure that what had begun in 1939 would not break down in 1970's. Times were changing. A new look was brought to the *Junior Historian* magazine and it was called the *Texas Historian,* the first issue coming out in September, 1970. Dr. Frantz observed that with the 18 year olds voting and having to serve in the army, teenagers did not want to be called junior any more. He summed it up by saying, "The Junior Historian has declared its manhood and independence. Don't call me junior any more; I'm a Texas historian now. . . ." Frantz went on to challenge the young writers and cautioned, "It's up to you to see that we live up to all that [the Texas Historian] promises and implies."

The first Junior Historian meeting was held on April 25,

1940. One of those Junior Historians attending the meeting wrote an account of what took place. I wish I could take credit for these next few lines since I owe so much to the Junior Historians and since these words express my sentiments:

> The meeting was called to order, thus launching the Junior Historian organization on its swift journey to greatness and fame. Dr. Walter Prescott Webb spoke to us as to our purpose and meaning. We shall not forget our mission though our work passes to others and we take our places in Texas and the world. We shall always be Junior Historians at heart.

Appendix

J. P. Bryan, 1965-1967
Seymour V. Connor, 1967-1968
Wayne Gard, 1968-1969
Rupert N. Richardson, 1969-1970
Cooper K. Ragan, 1970-1971
Dorman H. Winfrey, 1971-1972

editors, southwestern historical quarterly, 1897-1972

George P. Garrison, 1897-1910
Eugene C. Barker, 1910-1912
Eugene C. Barker and Herbert E. Bolton, 1913-1937
Rudolph L. Biesele, Charles W. Hackett, Walter P. Webb, 1937-1940
Walter P. Webb, Managing Editor; Rudolph Biesele, Charles W. Hackett and H. Bailey Carroll, Associate Editors; 1940-1943
Walter P. Webb and H. Bailey Carroll, 1943-1947
H. Bailey Carroll, 1947-1966
Joe B. Frantz, 1966-

publications of the texas state historical association

Adams, Ephraim Douglass, ed. *British Diplomatic Correspondence Concerning the Republic of Texas, 1828-1846.* Austin: The Texas State Historical Association, 1918. 636 p. OP

Erath, George Bernard. *Memoirs of George Bernard Erath.* Austin: The Texas State Historical Association, 1923. 105 p. OP

Carroll, H. Bailey. *Texas County Histories: A Bibliography.* Austin: The Texas State Historical Association, 1943. 200 p. OP

Schwettman, Martin W. *Santa Rita, The University of Texas Oil Discovery.* Austin: The Texas State Historical Association, 1943. 43 p.

Haley, J. Evetts. *Charles Schreiner, General Merchandise: the Story of a Country Store.* Austin: The Texas State Historical Association, 1944. 73 p. OP

Mosely, J. A. R. *The Presbyterian Church in Jefferson.* Austin: The Texas State Historical Association, 1946. 52 p. OP

Hawkins, Walace. *El Sal dey Rey: Fixing Title to Yo El Rey.* Austin: The Texas State Historical Association, 1947. 68 p. OP

Morton, Ohland, *Teran and Texas: A Chapter in Texas-Mexican Relations.* Austin: The Texas State Historical Association, 1948. 191 p. OP

Robinson, Duncan W. *Judge Robert McAlpin Williamson: Texas' Three-Legged Willie.* Austin: The Texas State Historical Association, 1948. 230 p.

Barker, Eugene C. *The Life of Stephen F. Austin: Founder of Texas; A Chapter in the Westward Movement of the Anglo-American People.* 2d ed. Austin: The Texas State Historical Association, 1949. 477 p. Originally published by Cokesbury Press, 1925.

Lathrop, Barnes F. *Migration into East Texas, 1835-1860.* Austin: The Texas State Historical Association, 1949, 114 p.

Winkler, Ernest W., ed. *Check List of Texas Imprints, 1846-1860.* Austin: The Texas State Historical Association, 1949. 352 p.

Cumulative Index of the Southwestern Historical Quarterly, Vols. I-XL, July, 1897-April, 1937. Austin: The Texas State Historical Association, 1950. 367 p.

St. Romain, Lillian Schiller. *A History of Western Falls, County, Texas.* Austin: The Texas State Historical Association, 1951. 160 p. OP

Eaves, Charles Dudley, and C. A. Hutchinson. *Post City, Texas.* Austin: The Texas State Historical Association, 1952. 171 p.

Webb, Walter Prescott, and H. Bailey Carroll, eds. *The Handbook of Texas.* 2 vols. Austin: The Texas State Historical Association, 1952. 1930 p.

Carroll, H. Bailey, and Milton R. Gutsch, compilers and editors. *Texas History Theses; A Check List of the Theses and Dissertations Relating to Texas History Accepted at The University of Texas, 1893-1951.* Austin: The Texas State Historical Association, 1955. 208 p.

Elliott, Claude, compiler and editor. *Theses on Texas History. A Check List of Theses and Dissertations in Texas History Produced in the Departments of History of Eighteen Texas Graduate Schools and Thirty-Three Graduate Schools Outside Texas, 1907-1952.* Austin: The Texas State Historical Association, 1955. 280 p.

Crouch, Carrie J. *A History of Young County, Texas.* Austin: The Texas State Historical Association, 1956. 326 p.

Stambaugh, J. Lee, and Lillian J. Stambaugh. *A History of Collin County, Texas.* Austin: The Texas State Historical Association, 1958. 303 p.

Connor, Seymour V. *The Peters Colony of Texas.* Austin: The Texas State Historical Association, 1959. 473 p.

Cumulative Index of the Southwestern Historical Quarterly, Vols. XLI-LX, July, 1937-April, 1957. Austin: The Texas State Historical Association, 1960. 574 p.

Barrett, Thomas. *The Great Hanging at Gainesville, Cooke County, Texas, October A. D. 1862.* Austin: The Texas State Historical Association, 1961. 34 p.

Carroll, H. Bailey, (and others). *The Junior Historian Movement in Texas; A Guidebook and a History.* Austin: The Texas State Historical Association, 1961. 111 p. OP

Diamond, George Washington. *George Washington Diamond's Account of the Great Hanging at Gainesville, 1862.* Edited by Sam Acheson and Julie Ann Hudson O'Connell. Austin: The Texas State Historical Association, 1963. 103 p. OP

Winkler, Ernest W., and Llerena B. Friend, editors. *Check List of Texas Imprints, 1861-1876.* Austin: The Texas State Historical Association, 1963. 734 p.

Scott, Zelma. *A History of Coryell County, Texas.* Austin: The Texas State Historical Association, 1965. 278 p.

Friend, Llerena, compiler and editor. *Talks on Texas Books, A Collection of Book Reviews by Walter Prescott Webb.* Austin: The Texas State Historical Association, 1970. 94 p. OP

Holden, William Curry. *The Espuela Land and Cattle Company; A Study of a Foreign-Owned Ranch in Texas.* Austin: The Texas State Historical Association, 1970, 268 p.

Barker, Nancy Nichols, compiler. *The French Legation in Texas.* Vol. I. Austin: The Texas State Historical Association, 1971. 357 p.

Pool, William C. *Eugene C. Barker: Historian.* Austin: The Texas State Historical Association, 1971. 228 p.

texas history paperbacks

Barker, Eugene C. *The Life of Stephen F. Austin: Founder of Texas, 1793-1836.*

Friend, Llerena B. *Sam Houston: The Great Designer.*

Hogan, William Ransom. *The Texas Republic: A Social and Economic History.*

Newcomb, Jr., W. W. *The Indians of Texas: From Prehistoric to Modern Times.*

Spratt, John Stricklin. *The Road To Spindletop: Economic Change in Texas, 1875-1901.*

Ramsdell, Charles William. *Reconstruction in Texas.*

Martin, Roscoe. *The People's Party in Texas: A Study in Third-Party Politics.*

Bolton, Herbert Eugene. *Texas in the Middle Eighteenth Century: Studies in Spanish Colonial History and Administration.*

Gantt, Jr., Fred. *The Chief Executive in Texas: A Study in Gubernatorial Leadership.*

Proctor, Ben H. *Not Without Honor: The Life of John H. Reagan.*

Soukup, James R., H. Clifton McCleskey, and Harry A. Holloway. *Party and Factional Division in Texas.*

Weddle, Robert S. *The San Saba Mission: Spanish Pivot in Texas.*

Gaillardet, Frederic. *Sketches of Early Texas and Louisiana.*

Wells, Tom Henderson. *Commodore Moore and the Texas Navy.*

Spell, Lota M. *Pioneer Printer: Samuel Bangs in Mexico and Texas.*